Moto G56
USER MANUAL

Tips, Tricks, and Troubleshooting

DALTON U. VICTOR

Copyright @ 2025 DALTON U. VICTOR

Legal Disclaimer

This user manual is an independent publication and is not affiliated with, endorsed, authorized, or sponsored by Motorola, Lenovo, or any of their affiliates. All product names, logos, and brands are property of their respective owners. The content is provided for educational and informational purposes only. While every effort has been made to ensure accuracy, the author and publisher are not liable for any damages or losses arising from the use or misuse of the information contained herein.

Table of Contents

Chapter 1

Introduction

About This Guide

Welcome to the Moto G56 User Manual: Tips, Tricks, and Troubleshooting! This guide is your comprehensive resource to understand and get the most out of your Moto G56 smartphone. If you're a first-time smartphone user or an experienced Android enthusiast, this manual will walk you through everything you need to know—from unboxing and initial setup to mastering advanced features and troubleshooting common issues.

The Moto G56 is packed with an array of features that enhance your smartphone experience, including a stunning 6.72" 120Hz display, a powerful MediaTek Dimensity 7060 processor, and the innovative Hello UI. This guide is designed to be both beginner-friendly and technically informative, with clear explanations and helpful tips. Throughout the manual, we'll cover key aspects of the device, including:

- Device setup and personalization
- Camera usage and photography tips

- Connectivity options like 5G, Wi-Fi 6, and Bluetooth
- Battery optimization strategies
- Security and privacy features
- App management and productivity tools

The goal of this guide is to empower you to take full advantage of your new Moto G56, regardless of your technical background.

How to Use This Manual

This manual is structured for easy navigation, with each chapter dedicated to specific aspects of the Moto G56. You can read it cover-to-cover for a thorough understanding, or use the table of contents to quickly find the information you need. Here's how to make the most of this guide:

- Step-by-step instructions: Whether you're setting up your device for the first time or adjusting settings later on, each section includes clear, actionable steps.
- Tips and Tricks: Special tips and pro recommendations are highlighted to help you unlock hidden features and optimize your Moto G56 experience.
- Troubleshooting: If you run into any issues, our troubleshooting sections will provide easy-to-follow solutions to common problems.

Transparency and Updates: Leaks vs. Final Specs

This guide is based on early leaks, rumors, and confirmed specifications available prior to the official release of the Moto G56. While we've worked hard to provide the most accurate and up-to-date information, please be aware that some features and specs may change when the final version of the device is officially launched. The Moto G56 may receive additional features or adjustments post-launch that are not reflected here.

To ensure that you have the most reliable information, we will update this guide periodically, especially after official announcements from Motorola. We strive to maintain the highest level of accuracy, but if there are discrepancies, they will be corrected in future versions of the guide.

Warranty & Support Information

Please note that this guide is unofficial and is not produced or endorsed by Motorola. The information in this manual is based on publicly available leaks, rumors, and early device specifications. As a result, any references to features or specifications may be subject to change.

If you need official support for your Moto G56, we recommend contacting Motorola directly. For warranty issues, product defects, or service inquiries, please refer to the official Motorola Support website or consult your device's warranty documentation.

Motorola's customer support can assist you with any hardware issues, software troubleshooting, or warranty claims. They offer support through various channels, including phone, email, and chat.

Please keep in mind that, as this is an unofficial manual, any warranty or product support related issues should be addressed with Motorola, not through this guide.

Chapter 2

Device Overview & Initial Setup

Unboxing Your Moto G56

Unboxing your Moto G56 is the first exciting step in getting to know your new device. Here's what you can expect to find inside the box:

- *Moto G56 smartphone* – The star of the show! Your sleek, powerful device.
- *USB-C Charging Cable* – For fast charging and data transfer.
- *Wall Charger* – Depending on your region, this may vary, but it supports rapid charging for the Moto G56.
- *SIM Ejector Tool* – Essential for inserting your SIM card and microSD card (if applicable).
- *Quick Start Guide* – A brief document providing a general overview of the device.
- *Warranty & Safety Information* – For reference, outlining the product's coverage and safety guidelines.

Before starting, ensure that everything listed above is in the box. If anything is missing or damaged, contact Motorola customer service right away.

Moto G56 Specifications

Here's a quick rundown of the key specifications of the Moto G56 that make it a standout smartphone:

Display, Processor, RAM, Storage

- *Display*: 6.72-inch IPS LCD, 120Hz refresh rate – Stunning, smooth visuals that are perfect for gaming, media consumption, and multitasking.
- *Processor:* MediaTek Dimensity 7060 – A powerful chipset that handles daily tasks with ease and delivers a strong performance for gaming and multitasking.
- *RAM:* 6GB or 8GB – Ample memory for smooth multitasking, ensuring your apps run fluidly without lag.
- *Storage:* 128GB or 256GB – Plenty of space for apps, photos, and videos. Plus, there's a microSD card slot for expansion.

Camera & Battery Details

- *Rear Camera:* 50MP dual-camera system – Capture detailed, high-quality photos, with support for night mode, portrait shots, and more.
- *Front Camera:* 16MP – Perfect for selfies and video calls, with AI-powered enhancements.

- *Battery:* 5200mAh – A large battery that ensures all-day performance. Paired with rapid charging, it will quickly recharge when needed.

First Time Setup

Once you've unboxed the Moto G56, it's time to power it on and set it up for the first time. Follow these steps to get started:

Turning On and Charging

- To power on the device, press and hold the Power button on the right side of the phone until the Motorola logo appears on the screen.
- If your phone doesn't power up right away, plug it into the included charger and allow it to charge for a few minutes before turning it on.
- You'll be greeted with a setup screen once the phone powers on.

Selecting Language & Region

- The first prompt on the screen will ask you to select your language and region. Use the on-screen keyboard to choose your preferred language.
- Afterward, select your region to ensure your phone's settings (like time zone and currency) are correct.

Setting Up Google & Moto Accounts

- Google Account: If you already have a Google account, enter your login credentials (email and password) to sign in. This will sync your Google apps, contacts, calendar, and settings.

- Moto Account: Motorola may also prompt you to sign into your Moto account, allowing you to access features like Moto Actions, Moto Display, and any device-specific perks.
- If you don't have a Google account, you can create one during this step.

Overview of the Hardware & Ports

Now that you've set up the basic settings, let's take a closer look at the Moto G56 hardware and physical ports:

Buttons, Fingerprint Scanner, SIM Slot

- Power Button: Located on the right side of the device, this button powers the phone on/off and is also used to lock/unlock the screen.
- Volume Buttons: Above the power button, these control the volume of your phone's audio.
- Fingerprint Scanner: Integrated into the Power button, it offers an added layer of security by allowing you to unlock your device with your fingerprint.
- SIM Card Slot: On the left side, there's a tray that holds both your SIM card and microSD card (if supported). Use the included SIM ejector tool to open the tray.

USB-C, MicroSD Slot, Headphone Jack

- USB-C Port: Located on the bottom, this port is used for charging the phone, data transfer, and connecting accessories like USB-C headphones or external devices.
- MicroSD Slot: The Moto G56 supports a microSD card for expanding your storage. This is especially helpful if you plan to store a lot of photos, videos, or apps.
- Headphone Jack: While many modern smartphones have removed this feature, the Moto G56 retains a 3.5mm headphone jack at the top of the device, allowing you to plug in your wired headphones.

Initial Configuration of System Settings

Now that the basics are set up, it's time to configure the system settings to suit your preferences:

Wi-Fi & Bluetooth Setup

- Wi-Fi Setup: The phone will prompt you to connect to a Wi-Fi network. Simply select your network, enter your password, and you're connected. A stable Wi-Fi connection is recommended for downloading apps and performing software updates.
- Bluetooth Setup: You can enable Bluetooth through the Settings menu. Once on, you can pair

the Moto G56 with Bluetooth devices like headphones, speakers, or smartwatches.

Date, Time, & Automatic Settings

- Automatic Date & Time: By default, the Moto G56 will automatically set the date and time based on your time zone. If you prefer, you can disable this option and set the date and time manually.
- Automatic Updates: Ensure your device is set to automatically download and install updates. This keeps your phone running smoothly with the latest security patches and improvements.

Display Settings

- Display Brightness: Adjust the brightness level by swiping down on the notification bar and using the slider. You can also enable Adaptive brightness for automatic adjustments based on your surroundings.
- Dark Mode: Moto G56 supports Dark Mode to reduce eye strain and save battery life. You can toggle this from the Display Settings or quickly enable it from the notification shade.

Congratulations! Your Moto G56 is now set up and ready to use. In the next chapters, we'll dive deeper into how to get the most out of your device, from exploring Android 15 features to camera tips and security settings. Stay tuned!

Chapter 3

Navigating Android 15 & Hello UI

What's New in Android 15

Android 15 brings a fresh and refined experience to the Moto G56, introducing a host of new features that make the device even more intuitive and efficient. Here are the most important updates you'll encounter:

- Refined User Interface: Android 15 enhances the smoothness of navigation with a more cohesive design. The system is faster and more responsive, offering a streamlined layout that's easy for both new and experienced users.
- Improved Notifications: Notifications are now more organized and interactive, allowing for quicker actions directly from the notification shade.
- Privacy Enhancements: With the introduction of new privacy options, Android 15 provides additional controls over app permissions, including a better view of what data each app can access.

- Better Multitasking: Android 15 allows for split-screen mode and enhanced app switching, making multitasking a breeze on the large 6.72-inch display of the Moto G56.
- Improved Dark Mode: The system-wide Dark Mode has been fine-tuned for less eye strain, and it also helps extend battery life.

Understanding Hello UI

Hello UI is Motorola's unique skin on top of Android 15 that brings both style and functionality. It includes several Moto-specific features that enhance the user experience. Let's explore how Hello UI customizes the Android experience:

Customization Options

One of the most appealing aspects of Hello UI is the ability to personalize your device. Here's how to make the Moto G56 truly yours:

- Widgets: Widgets are small app components that display information or quick controls directly on your Home Screen. To add a widget:
    1. Press and hold an empty space on your Home Screen.
    2. Tap Widgets in the menu that appears.
    3. Scroll through the available widgets, and drag the one you want to add to your Home Screen.

- Example: Add a weather widget to your screen to see the forecast without opening an app.
- Themes: Hello UI offers a variety of themes that allow you to change the overall appearance of your device, from icons to color schemes. To *change your theme:*
  1. Open Settings.
  2. Tap Display > Theme.
  3. Choose from the available themes or use a custom one.
- Example: Switch to a "Dark" theme for easier reading at night and to conserve battery life.
- Icon Packs: If you want a completely different look for your icons, you can download icon packs from the Google Play Store and apply them to your device. To change icons:
  1. Install an icon pack from the Play Store (e.g., "Moonrise Icon Pack").
  2. Open Settings > Display > Icon Pack and select your new pack.

Home Screen Management
Organizing your Home Screen is simple with Hello UI:
- App Folders: To create an app folder, press and hold an app icon, then drag it on top of another app. You can name the folder for easy access (e.g., "Social" for Facebook, Instagram, etc.).
- Changing App Icons & Shortcuts: You can tap and hold on an app to either remove it from the

Home Screen, move it to a different location, or add it to a folder. If you like, you can add a shortcut for quick access to specific functions of an app (e.g., a direct shortcut to a specific playlist on Spotify).

Advanced UI Customizations

For users who want to go beyond the basics, Android 15 and Hello UI offer plenty of customization options to make the Moto G56 truly your own.

Color Palette & Wallpaper Settings

- Color Palette: Under Settings > Display > Color Palette, you can adjust the color tone of your display. Whether you prefer warmer or cooler tones, you can tweak it to your liking.
- Wallpaper Settings: Change your wallpaper by going to Settings > Wallpaper & Style. You can choose from static images or dynamic wallpapers that change throughout the day. Moto G56 even supports live wallpapers to add some flair.

Icon Packs & Fonts

- Icon Packs: Beyond changing the theme, you can install icon packs from the Google Play Store for a complete makeover. Once installed, head to Settings > Display > Icon Pack to apply the new icons.
- Fonts: To change the font used on your device, go to Settings > Display > Font Style. Choose

from several available options, or download additional fonts from the Play Store.

Now that you know how to navigate Android 15 and Hello UI, customizing your Moto G56 becomes an exciting experience. From simple widget management to advanced theme setups, your device can reflect your style and preferences.

Chapter 4

Mastering Moto Gestures & Custom Features

Motorola's signature customizations are designed to make your interaction with the Moto G56 faster, smarter, and more intuitive. This chapter will guide you through the most popular Moto Gestures, Moto Display enhancements, and Moto Voice controls. Whether you want to snap a photo with a twist of your wrist or check messages discreetly without unlocking your phone, these features will streamline your experience.

Moto Actions Overview

Moto Actions are motion-based shortcuts that allow you to perform everyday tasks quickly. They're part of Motorola's exclusive software enhancements and are built to work without requiring full screen interaction.
Popular Moto Actions include:

- Chop Twice for Flashlight – Turn on the flashlight by making a double chopping motion with your phone.

- Twist to Launch Camera – Twist your wrist twice quickly to open the camera instantly.
- Pick Up to Silence – When your phone rings, simply picking it up silences the ringer.
- Flip for DND (Do Not Disturb) – Flip the phone face-down on a flat surface to silence all notifications.
- Swipe to Split – Swipe back and forth on the screen to activate split-screen mode (available in supported apps).

To access and manage Moto Actions:
1. Open the Moto app from your app drawer.
2. Tap on Moto Actions.
3. Toggle each gesture On or Off, and explore tutorials for how to perform them correctly.

Using Moto Display

Moto Display provides helpful information at a glance, without fully turning on the screen or draining your battery. It includes Peek Display, Always-On Display (Ambient Display), and lock screen enhancements.

Peek Display and Ambient Display

Peek Display uses motion sensors to detect when you approach or pick up the device. It softly illuminates the screen to show the time, battery status, and recent notifications.

Key Features:
- Interactive previews of notifications.

- Smart reply buttons for quick actions.
- Dims after a few seconds if there's no further interaction.

To enable Peek Display:
1. Open the Moto app.
2. Select Moto Display.
3. Turn on Peek Display and customize behavior (e.g., screen sensitivity, brightness level).

Ambient Display (Always-On) keeps a minimal info screen on when your phone is idle. You can toggle this *feature in:*
- Settings > Display > Lock Screen > Always-On Display

Notifications on Lock Screen
You can view, respond, or dismiss notifications right from the lock screen.
To customize lock screen notifications:
1. Go to Settings > Notifications > Lock Screen.
2. Choose from:
   - Show all notification content
   - Hide sensitive content
   - Don't show notifications at all

How to Activate and Use Moto Gestures

Here's a closer look at Motorola's two most popular gestures and how to activate and use them correctly.

Chop Twice for Flashlight

Use case: Need a light in the dark? No need to fumble with buttons.

To activate:

1. Open the Moto app.
2. Tap on Moto Actions > Chop Twice for Flashlight.
3. Toggle it On.

How to use:

- Hold the phone securely and make two quick downward chopping motions.
- The flashlight turns on/off with each double chop.

Troubleshooting Tips:

- Ensure your motion is firm but not aggressive.
- Don't have a tight grip—allow the accelerometer to detect movement.
- Restart the phone if the gesture becomes unresponsive.

Twist for Camera

Use case: Perfect for capturing moments quickly.

To activate:

1. Go to Moto Actions in the Moto app.
2. Toggle Twist for Quick Capture to On.

How to use:

- Hold the phone in your hand and twist your wrist twice quickly (like turning a doorknob).

Pro Tip: Works even when the screen is off.

Troubleshooting Tips:
- Try slower or faster wrist twists if the action doesn't register.
- Remove cases or accessories that may interfere with the motion sensor.

Setting Up Moto Voice

Moto Voice is Motorola's voice assistant that responds to custom wake commands and can perform specific tasks hands-free.

Setup Instructions:
1. Open the Moto app.
2. Select Moto Voice (if not available, download from the Play Store).
3. Follow on-screen instructions to:
    - Train your voice.
    - Set a custom launch phrase (e.g., "Hey Moto").
    - Grant microphone and background activity permissions.

Example Voice Commands:
- "What's the weather today?"
- "Open YouTube."
- "Set a timer for 10 minutes."
- "Text Mom: I'll call you later."

Troubleshooting Moto Voice:
- Voice Not Recognized: Re-train your voice in a quiet environment.

- Moto Voice Not Launching: Ensure battery optimization is turned off for Moto app.
- Doesn't Wake Up: Check microphone permissions under Settings > Apps > Moto Voice > Permissions.

With Moto Actions, Display, and Voice features, your Moto G56 becomes much more than a regular Android device—it becomes your assistant.

Chapter 5

Camera Usage & Photography Tips

The Moto G56 features a powerful 50MP dual-camera system designed to capture crisp, vibrant photos in nearly any lighting condition.

Overview of the 50MP Dual Rear Cameras

The Moto G56 is equipped with a 50MP primary sensor supported by a 2MP depth or macro sensor (depending on region). Together, they deliver clear daytime shots, enhanced low-light photography, and beautiful depth-of-field effects.

Key Features:

- 50MP Main Camera – High-resolution sensor for detail-rich photos.
- Depth/Macro Lens – For close-up shots or portrait-style bokeh effects.
- HDR (High Dynamic Range) – Automatically balances bright and dark areas.
- AI Scene Optimization – Detects scenes like food, landscapes, or text and auto-adjusts settings.

Camera App Interface & Settings

Once you open the Camera app, you'll see a clean, *user-friendly layout:*

Top Bar:

- Flash toggle (Auto / On / Off)
- Timer
- Aspect Ratio
- Settings gear icon (for resolution, watermark, shutter sound)

Bottom Carousel:

Swipe left or right to switch modes such as:

- Photo (default)
- Video
- Portrait
- Night Vision
- Macro
- Pro
- Slow Motion
- Time Lapse

Portrait Mode:

- Uses background blur to highlight your subject.
- Ideal for portraits, pets, or products.
- Tip: Tap the screen to adjust focus and lighting.

Night Mode:

- Brightens dark scenes without overexposure.
- Best used with a steady hand or tripod.
- AI boosts contrast and reduces noise.

Macro Mode:
- Ideal for objects less than 4cm away.
- Great for textures like leaves, fabrics, or close-up food shots.
- Avoid using in low light for best results.

Pro Mode:

Gives you manual control over:
- ISO (light sensitivity)
- Shutter Speed
- White Balance
- Focus Distance
- Exposure

Tip for beginners: Start experimenting with ISO and shutter speed in daylight before trying nighttime shots.

Taking Photos & Videos

Quick Capture Tips:
- Twist your wrist twice to launch the camera instantly (even when locked).
- Press Volume Button to snap a shot—great for selfies or stabilizing the phone.
- Tap to focus on a subject, then slide your finger up/down to adjust exposure.

Burst Mode:
- Hold the shutter button to capture a rapid sequence of shots.
- Ideal for sports, pets, or movement.

- The phone will help you pick the best frame, or you can choose manually.

Time Lapse:
- Compress hours of footage into seconds.
- Use a tripod or stable surface for best results.
- Great for sunsets, traffic, or clouds.

Pro Tip: For smoother videos, enable EIS (Electronic Image Stabilization) in the Video settings.

Editing Photos & Videos

Using Built-in Editing Tools:
- Open any photo in the Google Photos app (default gallery).
- Tap Edit (pencil icon) to access:
  - Crop/Rotate
  - Filters
  - Brightness/Contrast/Saturation
  - Portrait Light/Bokeh Blur Adjustments (for portrait mode photos)

Basic Workflow for Polished Photos:
1. Crop to improve composition.
2. Boost brightness slightly if underexposed.
3. Adjust contrast for better depth.
4. Use "Pop" filter to add vibrance without over-saturation.

Third-Party App Recommendations:
If you want more creative freedom:
- Snapseed – Pro-level editing with curves, lens blur, healing tool.
- Adobe Lightroom Mobile – For photographers who want to control tones, shadows, and light balance.
- VSCO – Stylish filters and advanced film-like color grading.

Selfies with the Front Camera

The Moto G56 front-facing camera is optimized for clear, natural selfies with skin tone balancing and beauty filters.

Best Practices:
- Use natural lighting (facing a window works wonders).
- Avoid zooming—step closer if needed.
- Enable Auto HDR for balanced tones.

Selfie Tips:
- Use the Timer to steady your hand and reduce shake.
- Palm Gesture: Raise your palm to trigger a countdown (if supported).
- Group Selfie Mode: Automatically adjusts field of view for wider group shots.

Pro Tip: In Portrait Selfie mode, use the depth slider to customize the level of background blur.

With practice, the Moto G56 camera becomes a reliable creative tool for capturing both everyday moments and artistic shots.

Chapter 6

Battery Life Optimization

With its robust 5200mAh battery, the Moto G56 is designed for all-day performance.
In this chapter, we'll break down power-saving features, smart settings, and charging best practices.

Understanding the 5200mAh Battery

The Moto G56's large 5200mAh battery is built to last:
- Up to 2 days of mixed use (manufacturer estimate)
- Fast charging supported via USB-C
- Integrated Battery Health AI (part of Android 15 & Hello UI)

Battery Highlights:
- Smart charge scheduling adapts over time to your usage patterns
- Long-life lithium polymer construction
- Deep integration with Adaptive Battery (covered below)

Power Saving Features

Battery Saver Mode

Battery Saver helps conserve energy by limiting background activity and reducing screen brightness when the battery is low.

To enable:

- Go to Settings > Battery > Battery Saver
- Toggle Use Battery Saver
- Optional: Set it to activate automatically at 15% or 20%

What it does:

- Pauses background syncing
- Reduces animations and visual effects
- Disables location access for non-essential apps

Adaptive Battery (Android 15 Feature)

Adaptive Battery uses AI to learn which apps you use most and limits power to those you rarely open.

Enable it here:

- Settings > Battery > Adaptive Preferences
- Toggle Adaptive Battery

Effect over time:

- Extends battery life based on usage patterns
- Prevents "rogue" apps from draining power in the background

Battery Health Management Tips

For long-term battery health:

- Avoid letting the battery drop below 10% regularly

- Unplug after fully charging—don't keep it on the charger overnight every day
- Use original or certified chargers to prevent overcharging or overheating
- Avoid charging during intensive gaming or video playback

Myth Busting:
- Myth: You must drain your battery completely before recharging.
  Truth: Modern batteries perform better with partial charges.

How to Optimize Battery Usage

App Battery Usage & Management
Monitor which apps use the most power:
1. Go to Settings > Battery > Battery Usage
2. See a ranked list of apps consuming power
3. Tap any app to restrict background usage

Tips:
- Social media, GPS, and streaming apps often top the list
- Limit auto-play, notifications, or background refreshes within app settings

Background Processes & Location Services
Restrict background activity:
- Settings > Apps > See All Apps
- Tap the app > Battery > Choose "Restricted" or "Optimized"

Disable high-drain services when not needed:
- Turn off Bluetooth, Wi-Fi, Mobile Data when not in use
- Use Airplane Mode overnight or when signal is weak (saves power)

Control Location Access:
- Settings > Location > App Permissions
- Set apps to "While Using" instead of "Always"

Pro Tips for Power Efficiency

- Use Dark Mode – Saves power on LCD/LED screens
- Lower Refresh Rate (if adjustable) – 120Hz is smooth, but 60Hz saves energy
- Auto-Brightness – Let the phone adjust based on ambient light
- Reduce Screen Timeout – Lower to 30 seconds or 1 minute

Chapter 7

Connectivity – 5G, Wi-Fi 6, Bluetooth, NFC

Modern smartphones are powerful because of their ability to connect seamlessly to networks, devices, and services. The Moto G56 supports high-speed 5G, ultra-fast Wi-Fi 6, Bluetooth 5.x, and NFC for contactless payments and smart device pairing.

5G and Wi-Fi 6 Setup

Activating 5G Network
Moto G56 supports Sub-6 5G bands, offering faster download speeds and lower latency.

To activate or check 5G:
1. Go to Settings > Network & Internet > Mobile Network
2. Tap Preferred Network Type
3. Select 5G/4G/3G (Auto)

Note: 5G availability depends on your carrier and location. You may need a 5G SIM card and plan.

Troubleshooting Tip:
- If 5G isn't working, try toggling Airplane Mode or restarting the phone.

- Make sure you're in a supported 5G coverage area.

Maximizing Wi-Fi 6 Speed & Performance

Wi-Fi 6 (802.11ax) is built for speed and efficiency, especially in crowded networks.

To connect to Wi-Fi 6:
1. Go to Settings > Network & Internet > Wi-Fi
2. Select your Wi-Fi 6 network (look for dual-band routers or "AX" label)
3. Enter the password and connect

Tips for Best Performance:
- Stay within a good range of your Wi-Fi router.
- Ensure your router supports Wi-Fi 6 (AX1800, AX3600, etc.).
- Avoid obstructions like walls or appliances.

Advanced Note:
Wi-Fi 6 may default to a 5GHz band—ideal for high-speed activities like streaming and gaming.

Bluetooth Connectivity

Pairing Devices & Troubleshooting
Bluetooth makes it easy to connect wireless headphones, speakers, smartwatches, and more.

To pair a device:
1. Swipe down > Tap the Bluetooth icon (or go to Settings > Connected Devices > Bluetooth)

2. Make sure the other device is in pairing mode
3. Select it from the list and confirm the pairing code

Troubleshooting Common Bluetooth Issues:

- Device not found? Make sure it's in pairing mode and close to your phone.
- Already paired but not connecting? Tap the device > Forget > Re-pair.
- Low audio quality? Toggle Bluetooth off/on or reset the connected device.

Using Bluetooth Audio & Wearables

Bluetooth supports:

- AAC and SBC audio codecs (for most wireless earbuds)
- Smartwatch sync (Moto Watch, Wear OS, etc.)
- Dual pairing (e.g., headphones + fitness tracker)

Battery Tip:

Disable Bluetooth when not in use to save power.

Using NFC for Payments & Pairing

NFC (Near Field Communication) lets you tap to pay, pair accessories, or share files.

Setting Up Google Pay

To enable NFC and use Google Pay:

1. Go to Settings > Connected Devices > Connection Preferences > NFC

2. Toggle NFC On
3. Download/open Google Wallet (Google Pay)
4. Add your credit/debit card and verify with your bank

To make a payment:
- Unlock your phone
- Hold it near the payment terminal
- Wait for vibration or confirmation

Payment Not Working?
- Make sure NFC is on
- Check that Google Pay is set as default
- Try re-adding the card

NFC Pairing for Devices & Accessories

Some wireless earbuds, speakers, or smart tags support tap-to-pair with NFC.

To use NFC pairing:
- Turn on NFC
- Tap your phone to the compatible device's pairing zone
- Follow on-screen prompts

Common Issues:
- No response? Check if the accessory supports NFC.
- Case interference? Remove thick or metal phone cases.

Final Tips & Troubleshooting Summary

Issue	Fix
5G not available	Confirm SIM + plan supports 5G; check network type settings
Wi-Fi 6 connection drops	Restart router; forget and reconnect to the network
Bluetooth device not pairing	Ensure close proximity; reset both phone and device
Google Pay errors	Verify NFC is on; re-add your card; check terminal compatibility

Chapter 8

Storage, RAM, & Virtual Memory Expansion

Internal Storage & MicroSD Expansion

Managing Storage Space

Your Moto G56 comes with 128GB or 256GB of built-in storage, depending on the model. Here's how to keep track and manage it:

To view your storage:

1. Go to Settings > Storage
2. You'll see a breakdown of space used by:
   - Apps
   - Photos & Videos
   - Audio
   - System
   - Cached data

Tips to free up space:

- Delete unused apps or games
- Clear download folders regularly
- Use cloud storage for media (e.g., Google Photos)

Moving Apps to SD Card

The Moto G56 supports microSD cards up to 1TB—perfect for photos, videos, and even apps.

To insert a microSD card:

1. Power off your phone
2. Use the SIM ejector tool to remove the SIM/microSD tray
3. Insert the microSD card, then reinsert the tray

To move apps to SD:

1. Go to Settings > Apps
2. Select the app > Tap Storage
3. If supported, tap Change > SD Card

Note: Not all apps can be moved. Core apps must stay in internal storage.

RAM Management & Performance Tuning

Activating Virtual RAM (RAM Boost)

Moto G56 comes with 6GB or 8GB of physical RAM, and supports RAM Boost (virtual memory expansion), allowing up to 4GB extra using internal storage.

To enable RAM Boost:

1. Go to Settings > System > Performance > RAM Boost
2. Toggle it On
3. Choose the additional RAM (e.g., +2GB or +4GB)

What it does: It temporarily uses storage space to help apps load faster and switch more smoothly.

Clearing Cache & Unused Apps

To clear cache for a specific app:
1. Go to Settings > Apps
2. Select the app > Storage & cache
3. Tap Clear Cache

To remove unused apps:
-   Go to Play Store > Manage Apps & Devices
-   Sort by Least used
-   Uninstall what you no longer need

Pro Tip: Avoid using "RAM Cleaner" apps—they can do more harm than good by force-closing background processes your phone needs.

File Management Tips

Organizing Files & Folders
Moto G56 includes a basic Files app, but you can use Google's own Files by Google for smarter suggestions and easy cleaning.

With Files by Google, you can:
-   Browse photos, downloads, and documents
-   Detect and delete duplicate files
-   Identify large files hogging space

To organize manually:
1. Open Files

2. Create folders like /Documents, /Screenshots, /Work
3. Move items using long-press > Move to

Using Google Files & Cloud Storage

Google Files app can back up to:

- Google Drive (for documents, PDFs)
- Google Photos (for unlimited photo backups at compressed quality)

To enable backups:

1. Open Google Photos > Settings > Backup
2. Choose backup quality and Wi-Fi preferences

Other cloud options:

- Dropbox
- Microsoft OneDrive
- Box

Offline Tip: Always move downloaded videos or podcasts to the SD card to keep internal memory clear.

Final Tips & Best Practices

Action	Why It Matters
Enable RAM Boost	Improves multitasking without slowing the phone

Move media to SD card	Frees up internal space and improves app performance
Clear cache monthly	Prevents bloated storage and laggy apps
Use Google Files cleaner	Offers smart cleanup suggestions without data loss

With smart storage management and RAM optimization, your Moto G56 stays fast, organized, and clutter-free.

Chapter 9

Security–Biometrics, Screen Lock, Permissions

Your Moto G56 is packed with advanced security tools to protect your data and maintain your privacy. This chapter will walk you through setting up fingerprint unlock, face recognition, screen lock types (PIN, Pattern, Password), app permission controls, Smart Lock, and other essential security features in Android 15.

Setting Up Fingerprint Unlock

Your Moto G56 includes a side-mounted fingerprint scanner integrated into the power button.

To set it up:

1. Go to Settings > Security & privacy > Fingerprint Unlock
2. Tap Add fingerprint
3. Set up a backup screen lock (PIN, pattern, or password) if not already done
4. Follow on-screen prompts to scan your fingerprint from various angles
5. Tap Done

Pro Tips:
- Register more than one finger for convenience (e.g., both thumbs)
- Clean the scanner regularly for better accuracy

Using Face Unlock

Face Unlock allows quick access just by looking at your screen, using the front-facing camera.

To enable Face Unlock:
1. Go to Settings > Security & privacy > Face Unlock
2. Tap Set up Face Unlock
3. Follow the camera prompt to scan your face in good lighting
4. Choose if face unlock works only when eyes are open (recommended)

Note: Face Unlock on Moto G56 is less secure than fingerprint/PIN. It's fast but can be bypassed by a photo or similar-looking person.

Screen Lock Options

PIN, Pattern, or Password

When you first set up fingerprint or face unlock, Android will require a backup lock type. You can always change it later:
1. Go to Settings > Security & privacy > Screen lock

2. Choose from:
    - PIN – 4+ digits (recommended for speed)
    - Pattern – connect-the-dots style
    - Password – combination of letters, numbers, symbols (most secure)

Biometrics vs. Password

Method	Security Level	Unlock Speed	Best For
Fingerprint	High	Fast	Daily use
Face Unlock	Medium	Fastest	Convenience
PIN/Password	Highest	Moderate	Extra protection/ data lock

App Permissions and Security Settings

Managing App Access to Data & Location

Android 15 gives you control over what apps can access, including your camera, microphone, contacts, and GPS.

To review app permissions:

1. Go to Settings > Privacy > Permission Manager
2. Tap categories like:
    - Location
    - Camera
    - Microphone
    - Files and media

3. For each app, choose:
    ○ Allow while using the app
    ○ Ask every time
    ○ Don't allow

Setting Up Two-Factor Authentication (2FA)

2FA is an extra layer of security for your Google account and apps like Gmail, WhatsApp, and banking apps.
To enable 2FA for your Google account:
1. Visit myaccount.google.com/security
2. Tap 2-Step Verification > Get Started
3. Add a backup method (e.g., SMS code or Google Authenticator app)

You'll now need your password and a second code to log in from a new device.

Bonus: Smart Lock & Lock Screen Privacy
Smart Lock allows your device to stay unlocked in trusted conditions:
- On-body detection – stays unlocked while you carry it
- Trusted places – stays unlocked at home or work
- Trusted devices – stays unlocked near your smartwatch or car Bluetooth

To enable:

1. Go to Settings > Security & privacy > Smart Lock
2. Choose your preferred unlock conditions

Lock Screen Privacy Settings:

Hide sensitive content like notifications on your lock screen.

To manage:

1. Go to Settings > Notifications > Lock Screen
2. Choose:
    - o Show all content
    - o Hide sensitive content
    - o Don't show notifications at all

Best Practices for Security

- Use fingerprint and strong PIN together
- Update your phone regularly to patch vulnerabilities
- Avoid installing apps from unknown sources
- Review app permissions monthly
- Enable Find My Device to track or erase if lost (Settings > Security)

Chapter 10

Apps Management & Productivity Tools

Pre-installed Apps Overview

Moto & Google Apps

Out of the box, your Moto G56 includes essential apps:

- Moto App – Customize gestures, display, and device behavior
- Moto Secure – Manage security settings and privacy tools
- Google Suite – Includes Gmail, Chrome, Google Maps, Google Photos, YouTube, and Google Drive

These are deeply integrated and essential for the full Android experience.

Third-Party Apps

Some regional versions may come with pre-installed apps (e.g., Facebook, Spotify). These can be disabled or uninstalled if not needed.

To disable/uninstall pre-installed apps:

1. Long-press the app icon
2. Tap App Info

3. Tap Uninstall or Disable

App Store: Google Play & Alternatives

Finding and Installing Apps

The Google Play Store is the primary and safest place to find apps.

To install an app:

1. Open Google Play Store
2. Use the search bar to find apps (e.g., "Zoom" or "Duolingo")
3. Tap Install

Updating Apps

Keeping apps updated ensures you get the latest features and security patches.

To update:

1. Open Google Play Store
2. Tap your profile icon > Manage apps & device
3. Tap Update All (or manually select)

Alternatives to Play Store

If needed, you can use:

- Amazon Appstore
- APKMirror (manual installs—use caution)
- OEM app stores (region-specific)

Warning: Avoid installing apps from unknown sources unless you trust the source. Always enable Play Protect (Settings > Security).

Productivity Features

Multitasking & Split-Screen Mode

Split-screen lets you use two apps at once—great for students or remote workers.

To use split-screen:

1. Open App 1
2. Swipe up to access Recent Apps
3. Tap the app icon above the preview
4. Select Split screen
5. Choose App 2

Examples:

- Watch a lecture on YouTube while taking notes in Google Docs
- Use WhatsApp while checking a spreadsheet

Pro Tip: Some apps like games or camera may not support split-screen.

Using Google Workspace

Moto G56 supports seamless use of Google Workspace (formerly G Suite):

- Gmail for business/personal email
- Google Calendar to manage tasks & meetings
- Docs, Sheets, and Slides for writing, spreadsheets, and presentations
- Google Meet for video calls

Example: School Scenario

- Access class notes via Google Drive

- Submit assignments through Google Classroom
- Join live sessions on Google Meet

Microsoft Tools

Prefer Office apps? You can easily install:

- Microsoft Word, Excel, PowerPoint
- OneDrive for cloud storage
- Microsoft Outlook for email
- Teams for work collaboration

Tips:

- Sign in with your school or work account
- Enable offline access for Docs/Excel
- Use OneNote for digital notebooks

Bonus: App Behavior & Background Management

To save battery and speed up performance, you may want to limit certain app behaviors.

Steps:

1. Go to Settings > Apps > See all apps
2. Tap on the app
3. Select Battery > Choose from:
   - Unrestricted – full access
   - Optimized – balance between use and battery
   - Restricted – limits background activity

Use restricted for apps you don't use often (e.g., delivery apps or games).

Chapter 11

Accessibility Features

The Moto G56 includes a comprehensive suite of accessibility tools designed to support users with visual, hearing, or mobility challenges.

Accessibility Settings Overview

You can access accessibility features by going to:

Settings > Accessibility

Here, you'll find tools grouped by need—vision, hearing, interaction, and audio & on-screen text.

Key Visual Support Features

- Magnification

  Lets you zoom into parts of the screen using gestures.

  To enable:

    - Go to Accessibility > Magnification
    - Choose from Tap button, Triple-tap screen, or Accessibility shortcut
    - Pinch and drag to zoom in/out.

- Font & Display Size

    - Text size: Adjust via Settings > Display > Font size

- Display size: Zoom the entire screen UI for easier viewing.
- Color Correction & Color Inversion
Useful for users with color blindness or contrast sensitivity.
    - Go to Accessibility > Color correction
    - Choose modes: Deuteranomaly (red-green), Protanomaly, or Tritanomaly
    - Color inversion flips colors for higher contrast (may affect media quality).

Hearing Support Tools
- Sound Amplifier
Boosts audio from media or surroundings via headphones.
    - Available via Accessibility > Sound Amplifier
    - Works best with wired or Bluetooth earbuds.
- Mono Audio & Balance
    - Ideal for users with hearing loss in one ear.
    - Adjust in Accessibility > Audio adjustment
- Hearing Aid Support
    - Connect Bluetooth-enabled hearing aids via Settings > Connected Devices
    - Look for the Hearing Aid label in supported models.

Using Voice Commands & Screen Reader

Google Assistant & Voice Access

- Google Assistant
  Allows full voice control: open apps, send messages, control smart home devices.
  To activate:
    - Press and hold the power button or say "Hey Google"
    - Enable from Settings > Apps > Assistant
- Voice Access
  Offers hands-free navigation with spoken commands.
  Steps:
    - Go to Accessibility > Voice Access
    - Toggle on "Use Voice Access"
    - Speak commands like "Scroll down" or "Open Gmail"

TalkBack & Magnification Gestures

- TalkBack
  Reads aloud what's on screen—great for users with visual impairments.
  To enable:
    - Go to Accessibility > TalkBack
    - Use gestures to navigate by touch while receiving spoken feedback
- Magnification Gestures
  As explained earlier, this lets you zoom in on content with three quick taps.

Tip: Use Accessibility Shortcut (bottom corner icon) for instant access to TalkBack or Magnification.

One-Handed Mode & Gesture Navigation

One-Handed Mode

- Shrinks the screen for easier thumb reach
- Especially helpful for users with motor limitations or smaller hands
  To enable:
- Go to Settings > System > Gestures > One-handed mode
- Swipe down in the center of the bottom edge to activate

Gesture Navigation

Gesture navigation simplifies control with intuitive swipes:

- Swipe up to go home
- Swipe from left/right edge to go back
- Swipe up and hold for recent apps

To switch or adjust:

- Go to Settings > System > Gestures > System Navigation

Chapter 12

Software Updates & Digital Wellbeing

Keeping Your Moto G56 Updated

Why Updates Matter
Software updates bring:
- Security patches to keep your data safe
- Bug fixes for better performance
- New Android features and Moto enhancements

How to Check for OTA (Over-the-Air) Updates
1. Go to Settings > System > System updates
2. Tap Check for updates
3. If an update is available, follow the on-screen steps
   - Connect to Wi-Fi and ensure battery is above 50% or plug in the charger
   - Don't interrupt the process—your phone will reboot automatically

Manual Installation (Advanced)
If you're not receiving updates normally, you can manually sideload using a PC:

- Visit Motorola's support site to download the latest firmware
- Use ADB tools and follow exact instructions (not recommended for beginners)
  Tip: Always back up your data first

Troubleshooting Update Issues
If your Moto G56 won't update:
- Not enough storage? Clear space in Settings > Storage
- Stuck in update loop? Restart into Safe Mode: Hold Power > Long-press "Power Off" > Tap OK
- Updates failing repeatedly? Perform a factory reset after backing up data

What's New in Android 15
Android 15 offers:
- Smarter battery optimization
- Revamped notification controls
- Improved privacy dashboards
- New multitasking animations and accessibility enhancements

Digital Wellbeing Tools

Digital Wellbeing helps you understand your screen habits and strike a healthier balance with your phone. You'll find these tools in:
Settings > Digital Wellbeing & Parental Controls
Screen Time & App Timers

- Dashboard: See how long you've used each app today
- Set app timers:
    - Tap an app > Choose daily limit (e.g., 1 hr/day)
    - Once the timer runs out, the app grays out until the next day

Pro Tip: Great for limiting social media, games, or YouTube browsing.

Focus Mode

Temporarily pause distracting apps while you work or study.

To activate:

1. Go to Digital Wellbeing > Focus Mode
2. Select apps to block (like Instagram or TikTok)
3. Schedule it or turn it on manually

You'll still receive important calls and texts—only distractions are silenced.

Bedtime Mode

Unplug and rest better with Bedtime Mode:

- Turns screen grayscale
- Silences notifications
- Optionally dims the wallpaper or enables Do Not Disturb

Set it up via:

- Digital Wellbeing > Bedtime Mode
- Sync with your Google Clock app or set custom hours

Bonus: You can link it to your charging schedule, so it kicks in automatically at night.

Chapter 13

Troubleshooting Common Issues

Even the best smartphones can hit a snag.

Device Not Turning On

Problem: Your Moto G56 doesn't power on.

Solutions:

1. Charge the Device
   - Plug the phone into a known working charger.
   - Wait at least 10–15 minutes—look for the battery charging icon.
   - If nothing appears, try a different cable or wall outlet.
2. Force Restart
   - Press and hold the Power and Volume Down buttons simultaneously for 20 seconds.
   - If the phone vibrates or shows a logo, it's restarting successfully.
3. Check for Physical Damage

- Inspect the charging port for dust or debris.
- If the phone was dropped recently, consider professional repair.

Prevention Tip: Avoid fully depleting the battery often; lithium batteries perform better with partial charges.

Connectivity Issues (Wi-Fi, Bluetooth, 5G)

Wi-Fi Not Connecting

- Toggle Wi-Fi Off/On in Quick Settings.
- Go to Settings > Network & Internet > Wi-Fi and forget the network, then reconnect.
- Restart both your phone and router.

Advanced: Reset network settings:

Settings > System > Reset options > Reset Wi-Fi, mobile & Bluetooth

Bluetooth Not Pairing

- Make sure the other device is in pairing mode.
- Remove old pairings: Settings > Connected devices > Previously connected devices
- Restart Bluetooth.

5G Not Working

- Ensure you're in a 5G-covered area.

- Go to Settings > Network & Internet > Mobile Network > Preferred Network Type, then select 5G.
- Restart the device.

Pro Tip: 5G drains battery faster—use 4G/LTE when 5G isn't essential.

Apps Crashing & Slow Performance

Apps Keep Crashing

- Force close the app:
  Settings > Apps > [App Name] > Force Stop
- Clear app cache/data:
  Settings > Apps > [App Name] > Storage & cache
- Update the app from Google Play Store.

Phone Feels Slow or Lags

- Restart the device.
- Remove unused apps: Settings > Apps > See all apps > Uninstall
- Enable RAM Boost: Settings > System > Performance Manager
- Free up storage: Settings > Storage

Pro Tip: Avoid live wallpapers and too many widgets—they consume memory.

Camera Issues & Fixes

Blurry or Unfocused Images
- Clean the lens gently with a microfiber cloth.
- Tap the screen to focus manually.

Camera App Won't Open or Freezes
1. Restart the phone.
2. Clear camera app cache:
   Settings > Apps > Camera > Storage & Cache > Clear Cache
3. Ensure no third-party camera apps are conflicting.

Photos Not Saving
- Check available storage.
- Grant storage permissions:
  Settings > Apps > Camera > Permissions > Files and Media

Screen, Display, and Touchscreen Problems

Unresponsive Screen
- Force restart: Press Power + Volume Down for 20 seconds.
- Remove any screen protector—some may block touch.
- Use Safe Mode to rule out app interference:

     o Hold Power > Tap and hold "Power Off" > Tap OK

Display Issues (Flickering, Lines, Black Screen)

- Adjust brightness: Settings > Display > Brightness level
- Disable Adaptive Brightness temporarily.
- If persistent, backup data and perform a factory reset as a last resort.

Prevention Tips for Common Issues

- Keep software updated: Settings > System > System updates
- Restart the phone once a week to refresh memory.
- Avoid installing too many background apps or battery optimizers.
- Use only certified accessories for charging and audio.

Chapter 14

Tips, Hidden Features & Long-Term Care

Hidden Features and Shortcuts

Custom Gestures & Quick Settings

Moto G56 includes gestures and shortcuts that go beyond the basics:

- Three-Finger Screenshot
  Swipe down on the screen with three fingers to take a screenshot instantly.
- Flip for DND
  Place the phone face-down on a flat surface to enable Do Not Disturb automatically.
- Lift to Unlock / Pick Up to Silence
  Enable these under Settings > Gestures to simplify unlocking or silence incoming calls with a simple motion.
- Quick Settings Panel Shortcuts
  Swipe down twice from the top to access the full panel. Tap the pencil icon to rearrange or add hidden toggles like:
  - Screen recorder

- ○ Focus mode
- ○ Dark theme
- ○ Extra dim (for low-light reading)

Pro Tip: Use "Quick Tap" (if enabled in Moto Actions) to double-tap the back of your phone and trigger a custom action like opening an app.

Secret Settings & Developer Options

Unlock Developer Options for advanced tweaks:

1. Go to Settings > About phone > Tap "Build number" seven times.
2. Developer Options will appear under Settings > System.

Popular tweaks include:

- Animation Scale Adjustments – Reduce lag by setting Window/Transition/Animator scales to 0.5x.
- Force Peak Refresh Rate – Useful on high-refresh screens (if supported).
- Limit Background Processes – Ideal for memory conservation.

Note: Be cautious—changing the wrong setting can affect performance or stability.

Long-Term Care & Device Maintenance

Treat your phone right and it'll go the distance. Here's how to preserve hardware and performance:

Screen Care
- Use a tempered glass screen protector to prevent cracks and scratches.
- Clean the screen gently using a microfiber cloth; avoid harsh chemicals.
- Be mindful of drops—invest in a shock-resistant case.

Replacing Parts
- Batteries and screens can be replaced, but it's best done by a certified technician.
- Avoid third-party parts unless they are OEM or Moto-certified.

Transferring Data from Your Previous Phone

Whether you're coming from Android or iPhone, Motorola makes transferring your data fast and simple using the Motorola Migrate tools or Google's built-in migration features.

From Android to Moto G56

1. During Initial Setup
   - Connect to Wi-Fi and sign in to your Google account.
   - Choose "Copy apps and data" when prompted.

- On your old phone, open Google's "Data Transfer Tool" (or follow on-screen QR code).
- Use a USB-C cable or Wi-Fi to connect the devices.
- Select what to transfer: apps, messages, photos, contacts, and more.

2. Post-Setup Option
   - Use Google Drive to back up your old phone (Settings > Google > Backup), then restore from backup on the Moto G56.

Pro Tip: Sign in to the same Google account to automatically sync contacts, calendar events, and even Chrome bookmarks.

From iPhone to Moto G56

1. On your iPhone:
   - Disable iMessage and FaceTime to avoid message disruptions.
   - Back up data to iCloud or a computer.
2. On the Moto G56:
   - During setup, choose "Copy from iPhone".
   - Use the Google Data Transfer tool and follow instructions to import:
     - Contacts (via iCloud login)
     - Photos and videos (via iCloud or Google Photos)

- Texts and call logs (limited)
- Apps (Android equivalents)

Important: Some apps may not transfer directly. You'll need to reinstall Android versions manually.

Cross-Platform Syncing Apps
If you skipped transfer during setup, you can use:
- Google One (cross-device backup)
- Send Anywhere, Xender, or ShareIt for file transfers
- Motorola Migration Assistant (in some regions)

www.ingramcontent.com/pod-product-compliance
Lightning Source LLC
LaVergne TN
LVHW010040070326
832903LV00071B/4439